MANDRILL

By Rachel Rose

Consultant: Darin Collins, DVM
Director, Animal Health Programs, Woodland Park Zoo

Minneapolis, Minnesota

Credits

Cover and title page, © John Gaffen/Alamy; 3, © Marlin's photos/Shutterstock; 4–5, © kuritafsheen/Getty; 6, © GlobalP/iStock; 7, © Photoshopped/iStock; 9, © Curioso.Photography/Shutterstock; 10–11, © IrinaFuks/iStock; 13, © iStock/Freder; 14, © Africa Studio/Shutterstock, © schankz/Shutterstock; 15, © Gleb__Ivanov/iStock; 16–17, © Amihays/Shutterstock; 18, © DikkyOesin/iStock; 19, © Abeselom Zerit/Shutterstock; 21, © picture alliance/Getty; 23, © stefbennett/iStock

President: Jen Jenson
Director of Product Development: Spencer Brinker
Senior Editor: Allison Juda
Associate Editor: Charly Haley
Designer: Colin O'Dea

Library of Congress Cataloging-in-Publication Data

Names: Rose, Rachel, 1968- author.

Title: Mandrill / by Rachel Rose.

Description: Minneapolis, Minnesota : Bearport Publishing Company, [2022] |
  Series: Library of awesome animals | Includes bibliographical references
  and index.

Identifiers: LCCN 2020058673 (print) | LCCN 2020058674 (ebook) | ISBN
  9781636911427 (library binding) | ISBN 9781636911502 (paperback) | ISBN
  9781636911588 (ebook)

Subjects: LCSH: Mandrill--Juvenile literature.

Classification: LCC QL737.P93 R67 2022 (print) | LCC QL737.P93 (ebook) |
  DDC 599.8/6--dc23

LC record available at https://lccn.loc.gov/2020058673

LC ebook record available at https://lccn.loc.gov/2020058674

Copyright © 2022 Bearport Publishing Company. All rights reserved. No part of this publication may be reproduced in whole or in part, stored in any retrieval system, or transmitted in any form or by any means, electronic, mechanical, photocopying, recording, or otherwise, without written permission from the publisher.

For more information, write to Bearport Publishing, 5357 Penn Avenue South, Minneapolis, MN 55419. Printed in the United States of America.

Contents

Awesome Mandrills! 4
Up, Down, and All Around. 6
The Biggest and Brightest 8
Hunted 10
Watch Out, or I'll Yawn! 12
Snack Time. 14
Many Mandrills 16
Time to Mate 18
Moms Know Best 20

Information Station 22
Glossary 23
Index 24
Read More 24
Learn More Online 24
About the Author...................... 24

AWESOME
Mandrills!

EEEK, EEK! A mandrill opens its bright-red mouth and lets out a scream. Big, loud, and colorful, mandrills are awesome!

MANDRILLS MAKE SOUNDS, SUCH AS SCREAMS AND LOUD GRUNTS, TO **COMMUNICATE** WITH ONE ANOTHER.

Up, Down, and All Around

The mandrills' cries can be heard in the rain forest. They make their homes among the trees in parts of Africa that are near the **equator**. By day, mandrills walk along the forest floor. When night falls, they climb up into trees. They find a different tree to sleep in each night.

WHEN MANDRILLS WALK, THEY PLANT THEIR BACK FEET FLAT BUT WALK ON THEIR FINGERS WITH THEIR FRONT FEET.

The Biggest and Brightest

Mandrills are the largest members of the monkey family. They are also some of the most colorful. A mandrill's long, red nose and blue cheeks make it stand out from other monkeys. So does its short, yellow beard. But a mandrill's face isn't its only colorful body part. Its bottom can be red, pink, or blue. **WOW!**

MALE MANDRILLS CAN WEIGH ABOUT 60 POUNDS (27 KG). FEMALES ARE ABOUT HALF THE SIZE OF MALES.

Hunted

Colorful rumps help mandrills keep track of one another in the forest. They can easily spot a bright-blue behind in front of them! Mandrills live in groups called troops. Staying close together helps to keep them safe. Big cats, large snakes, and **raptors** may attack mandrills.

MANDRILLS MAY SOON BECOME **ENDANGERED** BECAUSE OF THE HARM HUMANS ARE DOING TO THEIR FOREST HOMES.

Humans also hunt the colorful monkeys for their meat. In addition, humans are harming the rain forests where the animals live.

Watch Out, or I'll Yawn!

If a mandrill is faced with a **threat**, it may do something drastic—yawn. Wait, what?! Yawning allows a mandrill to show off its long, sharp teeth. It's a warning to **predators** to stay away.

An angry mandrill might also slap the ground. **SMACK!** With arms as big and strong as the mighty mandrill's, these slaps are a pretty clear sign to leave the monkey alone.

WHEN A MANDRILL IS NOT IN HARM'S WAY, SHOWING ITS TEETH CAN BE A FRIENDLY GREETING.

Snack Time

When they are not scaring away unwanted visitors, mandrills are looking for their own **prey**. They search the forest for ants, lizards, frogs, and snails. **YUM!** But much of their **diet** is made up of fruit, nuts, and seeds.

MANDRILLS ARE PRETTY HANDY—LITERALLY. UNLIKE MOST ANIMALS, THEY USE THEIR FINGERS TO GATHER FOOD.

Many Mandrills

Male mandrills spend most of their time hunting for food. Usually, they do this on the ground and alone. Females and their young find food in the trees. When they aren't eating, mandrills take turns **grooming** one another.

THERE ARE AROUND 40 MANDRILLS IN A TROOP. BUT AS MANY AS 1,200 MANDRILLS MAY COME TOGETHER AT A TIME.

Time to Mate

There is usually one male in charge of each troop. Males fight to be in the top spot because when it is time to have young, female mandrills pick the strongest male. They usually **mate** between July and October. After six months, baby mandrills are born.

THE STRONGEST MALE MANDRILLS ARE THE MOST COLORFUL.

Moms Know Best

For the first few days, newborn mandrills hang on to their mothers' bellies. Then, they travel on their mothers' backs. New mothers keep their babies close for about a year and a half.

Female mandrills are fully grown when they are four to seven years old. Males take up to nine years to grow. Then, they are ready to start families of their own.

MANDRILLS IN THE WILD CAN LIVE UNTIL THEY ARE AROUND 30 YEARS OLD.

Information Station

MANDRILLS ARE AWESOME!
LET'S LEARN EVEN MORE ABOUT THEM.

Kind of animal: Like all monkeys, mandrills are mammals. Most mammals have fur, give birth to live young, and drink milk from their mothers as babies.

Other monkeys: Mandrills are part of the Old World Monkey family, which is made up of more than 130 **species**. Baboons are in the same family.

Size: Male mandrills are about 2.4–3 feet (75–95 cm) long. That is about as big as a large dog.

MANDRILLS AROUND THE WORLD

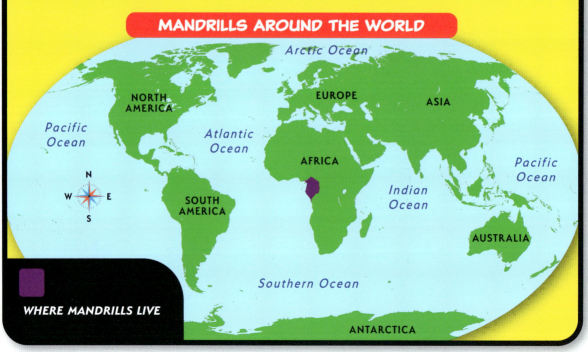

WHERE MANDRILLS LIVE

22

Glossary

communicate to share information, ideas, feelings, and thoughts

diet the kind of food a person or an animal eats

endangered being in danger of dying out

equator the imaginary line around the middle of Earth

females mandrills who can give birth to young

grooming cleaning by removing dirt, insects, dead skin, and tangled fur

male a mandrill that cannot give birth to young

mate to come together in order to have young

predators animals that hunt and kill other animals for food

prey an animal that is hunted and eaten by other animals

species groups that animals are divided into according to similar characteristics

threat someone or something that might cause harm

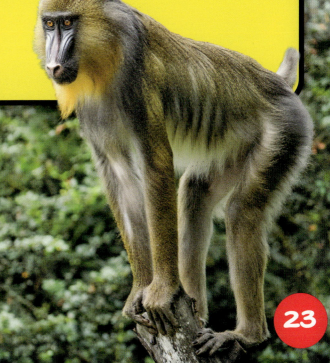

Index

Africa 6, 22
baby 18, 20
colors 4, 8, 10, 18
equator 6
food 14, 16
humans 10–11
mate 18

monkey 8, 12, 22
predators 12
prey 14
rain forest 6, 11
teeth 12–13
threat 12
troops 10, 16, 18

Read More

Bodden, Valerie. *Monkeys (Amazing Animals).* Mankato, MN: Creative Education, 2020.

Kenney, Karen Latchana. *Monkey Troops (Better Together: Animal Groups).* Minneapolis: Jump!, 2020.

Learn More Online

1. Go to **www.factsurfer.com**
2. Enter "**Mandrill**" into the search box.
3. Click on the cover of this book to see a list of websites.

About the Author

Rachel Rose writes books for children, and she teaches yoga. She lives in San Francisco with her husband and her dog, Sandy.